A UNIVERSE OF
BROKEN MATTERS

OMG, I will miss
this smiley face a lot
but yeah we we'll keep
in touch girl. Thanks
for always being super
- nice and helping
me review some
of these poems
you are a wonderful
person

♡

A Universe of Broken Matters

Poems from the heart

by Windila Balbone

Published by Windila Balbone

Bronx, NY 10457

Website: windilabalbone.com

Email: windila.balbone@gmail.com

Image credits:
page 9: *Lost* by TheFoxAndTheRaven
page 17: *Black Rose* by star boy
page 21: *Broken Face* by Argief
page 25: *Broken Window* by Ryan McGilchrist
page 43: *Skidrow LA* by Jorobeq at English Wikipedia
page 55: *Two Hands* by Windila Balbone
page 61: *Night* by Windila Balbone
page 65: *Pillow* by Windila Balbone

First printing: August 2017

ISBN-13: 978-1548738877

Dedication

To all my International Community High School lovely teachers and counselors who bring out the best of us and show their belief in what we can do. I can never thank you enough.

To my LIT (Leadership in Training) and my BTO (Beat the Odds) family

To all my family members, my friends and especially my mother for the support and the sacrifice to make me who I am.

Finally, to all the suffering, unfortunate souls that live under the storms. Your voice will be heard.

Internal Conflict

Lost

I am walking down the aisle

Carrying a light bundle but a heavy burden and a painful one

I am walking Down the aisle. There are not roses, it is not pink,

but it is gloomy

Dark. Still waiting for the last rain drop

Still waiting for a rescue that will heal my heart

Still begging to live

Still wanting the pieces of my heart to be put together

Even if it will never be the same again

I am walking Down the aisle not the joyful one

but the sorrowful one

No father to walk me in but a broken heart to tear me apart

Not a healing soul have found me yet

But I won't stop walking Down the aisle that might not have a

limit

<u>Self</u>

I'm sure that you look at yourself

in the mirror and hate what you see

You wish you could be the girl in the school that

has all the boys at her knees

You tell yourself I wish I was beautiful like her

I wish I did not have to go through all this pains and hardship

But guess what

The girl that you see there, she is living day to day under the

domination of fear behind a charade.

Because she can't show her true self

She has to hide behind her physical appearance

People do not love her because of who she is on

the inside but they love her for what they see

Don't wish to be her

Love yourself, learn to embrace your uniqueness

Don't wish to have everything easily because life is not a fairytale

It is a battlefield and the winners are the ones that fight

to be more strong, powerful in the inside, the outside, emotionally

To have the power to hope, to survive, for determination

They are the winner and none will bring you there

if you don't stop wishing to be someone else and learn that they

can't be you.

Let it out

It hurts to open up

But it also destroys to keep closed up

Either way, it will feel like a penitentiary

Or being dead in the water.

You don't find your true self unless you

Let all the unspoken words and fears out. But to whom?

 Opening up is fearful in such

A self-destructive universe

It is like exposing your naked self to individuals that

You will never know enough

With sometimes two faces, spurious, smiley faces with bloody

inflamed hearts

It breaks you down like you were made of clay

We don't open up because we hurt each other

Because we deceive each other

Because your sadness will make most happy

We don't because we do not have faith and trust

The only things that can truly save our souls

Bittersweet

My life is bittersweet

It is like a butterfly flying everywhere

Contemplating the beauty of nature

In vain to find a flower to settle down

It sometimes turns into an unreachable skyscraper

made of paper that can slump anytime

That hopes, that is determined, that inspires to last longer

Even if it knows that it can't

I have no clue who I am, Where I can fit

In one place I'm goofy, smiling and speaks out my mind

 In the other, I feel like a cat got my tongue. Who am I ?

My life is a pattern of seasons with still the same purpose trying

to find who I am

Trying to find a response when someone asks who are you in this

life?

Remembering

Sometimes, it takes a small tiny thing, a place,

A song, an action, a name to bring back

 all the destructive memories and sometimes the good ones

But we all know that the sad ones stay longer

Because they hurt more

They are like holes in our heart, that can stop us from breathing

We sometime try to forget them because we regret them

Because we can't travel back in time to fix them

We wish they could be erased from our minds

Because they are sad songs that break

down like flower petals.

They can create open wounds that take a long time to heal again

And the idea that they will always be...

there at a certain moment in our life, any moment

Kills as in a battlefield.

But what can we do about it? They are part of us.

<u>Did you know</u>

Did you know that I'm crying inside and outside

Blaming myself, hating myself for

Thinking about something that

Will never exist, or so I believe

While you are maybe in a different space

Moving on, open to a different life

Did you know that I regret that I did not open up

That I closed up and did not let you in

I am crawling because

the pieces of my heart are burning down living ashes

that I am still trying to wash away

Did you know that the blue sky seems to be a dark infinite tornado when I am alone

Little do you know I am fading away because of depression that has become my home

Based on *Little Do You Know* by Alex and Sierra

The neglected one

The one who is always to be replaced

The one who everyone turns to when all doors close

The one to whom they give their back

when they find better somewhere else

The one who will stand for them, will please them

Also the one for whom they will never care so much

The one whose smile is so bright and dazzling

Just as the hidden pain behind this smile is so tense and lonely

The one that wishes she could be treated the way she treats them

<u>Behind curtains</u>

We hide behind curtains

Seeking freedom

Afraid to let them know

Afraid that they will judge us

Afraid that we will be disappointment to them

Afraid they won't accept us

We sacrifice our freedom and happiness

Because we don't want to lose them

We sometimes let out pieces of our true selves as hints

Sadly, it is senseless for them

All we need is to let it out

 all we want is to shout out to the entire world

Because all it takes is boldness, courage

Because we will never know unless we try

And we will survive for that day when

we show our true self and vulnerability.

13

__broken__

Broken windows

Shattered soul

Made me mad and empty

Made me desperate

Let you in, let you destroy the last pieces

And fade away

Because it was my choice not to face you.

Knowing that everyday will be full

Be full of tired and phony happiness

And every night will be longer, lonely, tearful

With wretched thoughts

The Bride of Loneliness

I am the bride of loneliness

Like an abandoned and haunted house

I attract boredom and melancholy

I am like a poisonous rose that at the smell of my perfume makes

You sleep like sleeping beauty

I see things in a old fashion not like the others

I am the bride of loneliness and it is hard

To defeat my union because it is my personal zone.

I made a pact with it.

Forgetting

Sometimes, it takes forgetting to build happiness

But it is ridiculously hard to forget

To even think of forgetting

Because every moment that you think about it,

It hurts more, it is painful

That's the thing that makes you want to forget

You want to forget so bad but nothing is going away

You wonder if it is the heart, the spirit or the mind

You pretend to forget but the imagination is still around the

Thing you wish to forget

Forgetting can be a really harmful poison

That kills you little by little

Because the word itself makes you remember what you

Wish to forget

But one thing is sure .Forgetting is helpful

 when it heals your soul and heals you from sorrow

<u>She told me</u>

I told her don't cry.

Everything will be fine

Without even knowing what happened

She said it is not that easy.

You can't understand

I wandered and wondered for the rest of the time

What she meant

Until I grew up. Now

I understand but I am still

Trying to figure it out.

Because of her. I am trapped in the same labyrinth

Unlike

Unlike many, Ze* was raised not to show zir feelings but a

blank, non harmful,

Supposed to be strong face.

Unlike many, Ze was raised not to trust anyone around zir

To let things sink in deep and build a box full of them

And maybe wait for the blowup day

Unlike many, zir entire life was made of doubts,

It was built up in the roots of insecurities, lack of confidence,

silence

Ze was always the second choice

Ze was never the favorite

Zir heart was full of misery

Ze thought that was being strong

Now Ze has to face it all.in a stumbling world

Ze feels weak, unworthy, senseless.

20

Zir heart is full of misery

Unfortunately for zir, these circumstances did not lead zir into

the positive way

It is hard for zir to get out

From what society has made of zir

*Ze IS used for gender neutral and Zir is used for gender

neutral possession.

External Conflict

Woman

Too fat Too thin

Too chubby Too fake

Too simple, A tomboy. Ugly

Nowhere to fit in but still trying to fit in

That's the struggle, those are the words that we have

to hear every day of our life

Why do you make it ok to objectify me?

Why do you make it ok to blame the victim

of a rape because of their choice of clothes?

You call me unconfident because I wear makeup

You slut shame me but you accept a playboy

I started to believe you, to believe that I was inferior and

that's where I am supposed to be

because you said it loud enough, big enough.

But guess what, you cannot stop me anymore

I am hungry for freedom, I am eager for equality and respect

I am craving for education. I am an enraged storm

That won't stop unless the rain starts and the rainbow of liberty

erases my anger.

I am not different

Being an immigrant does not make me different.

It does not make me less than you

It is not illegal because I am a human being

Why do I have to survive under fear of you

Under fear when I already ran away from fear

Why do you condemn me into the dusk

until I stop reaching for the sunlight?

Being an immigrant is just a matter of paper

Not my life, not my character, not my personality.

It should not mean that I am a criminal, that I am violent

When I am just trying to find my way to the light

Do not label me because you will never encounter

 the monstrous fear that I fought

You might not even be able to survive 1 minute of my life

I am Windila, an immigrant here for the rise of hope, here to

shine.

Like many, my fight won't stop until ignorance vanishes

I am not a criminal, I dream high and I believe strongly

Let me be, Let us breathe. Aren't we all humans on mother

earth?

Black women

They tell me that I'm fake, I'm violent, a hussy,

But in reality I'm none of those

In reality I'm trying to be authentic in a society full of copies

They tell us that we are not attractive at all,

That I need to take off my weave, be natural

When I do so,

They call me nappy hair, weird, can I touch your hair?

It is not my fault if I can pull everything and rock it (black hair

magic)

They created a single story of us. They labeled us as

 Being tough, loud, harsh, masculine, angry... all that

They said it loud, they said it big enough and a lot

But I say they are confusing themselves between someone

that is speaking out her mind for the right thing and

someone that speaks not to say anything

I say that's what makes us unique, powerful, strong

They call me, big nose, big lips, too dark.

You need to fix yourself

I say it is not my fault if my melanin is popping

like a shining star

I ask why are big lips attractive and celebrated

in a white woman that fakes it

but ugly in a black woman that embraces her natural beauty?

Let us be

Society

You tell us that we are free but still hold our freedom tight

beneath your hands

We stumble, We endure all your challenges day to day until

our lives becomes living hells and dying is the only way to find

peace. But We still find a reason to live

You tell us to be united, to fight for our rights, for equality

But what equality are we talking about? Rip all the papers with

equality, liberty on it because equality isn't equality if the fruits of

change still look down miserably at each other.

If some sleep on a rocky pillow and some on a smooth one.

Freedom is not freedom, Peace of mind isn't

If my thoughts, my beliefs, my appearance and my life are a

danger to yours

If you label me and force me into a ox that works for you

When what we truly need is equity but you can't see beyond your

desire, society

What a hypocrite are you? What a beast are you. Society

You are a self-destructive monster.

You are so lost that your individuals are no longer valued based

on ethics and morality

but by looks, by likes, by comments.

You call for peace but you enflame wars, death of innocents

You said that education is the only way to put a light in our

lives but what is education when you limit your people?

All you create is ignorance, hate among your people.

Stop it, stop it, stop it and stop it society, wake up society, wake

up people because society is you, it is me, it is us and the only

thing that gets in our way is us.

America

Your people are being torn apart but you stayed

blind and mute in front of that

They are screaming, fighting

But you still seem to be blind-folded

The world is begging you to stop

But you are getting more and more self-destructive.

You destroyed everything, the lives of your people,

of innocents for insignificant values

You made yourself full of ignorance, controversies.

You arise fast, strongly, with determination

But do not forget that you can get low, come down

And not be able to see which way is up

Remember the blood of those that fought for your independence

Don't let it be for granted

Remember those that were torn apart from their families

Not because they wanted but they were forced to

Remember their decades of suffering

Remember those that saw their land stolen away

Don't fool yourself, don't fool your people

Remember how great you are seen in the eyes of

 the people living in the other parts of the world

America you know that the world expects a lot from you

But not just a trashy bag full of smelly hates, resentment,

fascism, racism , xenophobia, islamophobia.

You know you are more than that.

It is not too late America, for the future, for your kids,

For the fathers whose blood fed our freedom to grow.

Who am I to judge him

Who am I to look at him with disgust when I am not different

Well we all have stereotypes.

My first impression was he is gross, ugly,

 must be a criminal, dangerous

Why all these piercings? Because we were

 not different but we had different styles

But I still sat facing him because of no other choice

Still scared of his disgusting look and all the weird stuff that I

could

Not even describe. Then something unexpected happened

A smile. I smiled and got a sincere smile back

Then I realized I was wrong the whole time

For judging and labeling him

I felt sorry for him but for me too because

I did not know him

Yet I had already put him in the box of criminals

The stranger

I saw him in the train

Really self -conscious

I want to tell him that he is beautiful, handsome the way he is

That I won't judge him

That I see him just as I see other people

That he is not different from others

That I can read a kind heart in his dazzling eyes

That he doesn't need to feel like vanishing

That his scars, his burns, his flaws are what make him

I wish I could be strong enough to tell him

But he is just a stranger to me

And saying it will only remind him that he has those scars

The guy in the train

The streets

The streets are cold, they are freezing

Their trees are freezing

The leaves are dry , loose, falling

The houses are sorrowful and empty yet still full of pride,

families and small happiness

Their minds are wandering in the storm of desperation

The street smells of misery, sadness, dirt, trash in their faces

Tired of slavery, tired of mountains of bills lack of sleep but won't

stop

They all came and are here for the sun light to rise

What will it take to rise?

<u>I am not just a pretty girl</u>

I am not a toy. I am not an artistic work to admire

I am not just sweet. I should not always have to be submissive

I am not just a thing that should be catcalled

I am not just made to love pink and play with Barbie dolls

When I tell you I don't need your help, I truly don't need it

When I put on my makeup it is not to please you

Don't feel obligated to open the door for me or help me

I am not just made to bear kids

I am more than anything that you can ever think of

My heart is not made of rock, I have feelings, I can get hurt

I am a human being, I have respect for myself and I deserve to

be respected

I can be tough as I want, I can be creative, wild, as I want

I can be a girly girl and a tomboy if I want to

Don't put me in a box

I am a badass

I don't belong to anyone but myself. Do not make my decisions in

my place

I am not just a pretty girl, I am a hardworking human,

I am valuable, I have principles.

I am inspirational, brave

I used to play with cars

My true self is in my intellectuality and heart not in my

appearance

Pink was never my favorite color as you think

Coming out

The issue with gender expectations is that they divide us and push us to fit in a way that we don't want to, like the fact that men should be tough strong, not show their feelings, while women should be sweet, docile, fragile. It is not ok at all. Keeping those feelings kills, being docile enslaves us. Let's all be free, let's all break the walls of gender, escape from the fitting box, to find our true selves and freedom.

Relationship Issues

Why

Why did you say it, if you didn't mean it?

Why did you say it if you were not going to stay?

I still remember it

The "I miss you" that you sent

Were you afraid to hurt me?

Well you did

The harm is already done

because you waited

because you gave me high hope

So all these plans ended up like wretched skyscrapers.

I was your next mistake

I don't feel sorry for us, for you.

I feel sorry that I let you see

The part of me that I never show

because I trusted all your words, when you said

Nunca sera adios. (It will never be goodbye)

Too late. It is happening

My mistake I rushed, my mistake I did not wait

As you said it good things happen to those who wait.

From now, I am learning to wait.

Maybe

Maybe we were made to be like the sun and the moon

To always run away from each other but

Love one another despite thousands of impossibilities

Maybe we were made to be earth and sky.

To always see and feel each other's presence,

see what we have in the eyes of each other but

Never make it to the end because we are unbounded

And cry rivers of tears to show our desperation

Just like sky cries for earth

Or like water and fire. Be each other's medicine

Maybe like the wolf that always howls at nights

Probably looking for the other half

That might be howling somewhere else

They both know they are looking for each other

Even if the certainty of finding one another is almost impossible

They still have that hope.

Maybe the wolf is not calling a different wolf

Maybe the one thing that it needs is just right there

The moon but the wolf doesn't seem to realize it because it is

unreachable but who knows. Far or close, we must find our ways

The mystery

She was the rainbow to you

The harmonious one with many layers

She was a mystery to your eyes

You tried to read her

You tried to read her smile, her

Tears but you weren't brave enough to go beyond her storms

You wondered who she truly was

You couldn't find it

She is and still remains a mystery to you

<u>*Amnesia*</u>

I wanna wake up one morning and feel like all was a dream

Believe that I don't need someone to be fulfilled

See that I am happy with who I am

That I stopped thinking for all these years

That I decided to wake up

And actually did and I no longer look at your photograph

That I stopped being a stalker

That nothing bothered my mind

But just the idea of thinking about wishing that

*it was a dream, reminds me of how tattooed you are in my mind
and heart.*

He said

He said I will love you until my last breath

She responded, I am broken, I can't be loved

He was lost,

She said I am not ready to be loved.

I don't show myself enough love, I don't know which way to love

myself

How can I deserve someone's love? How can I love you back

To destroy you? To give you high hopes of a blank future?

I can't allow myself to put you through this.

I can't define love, I can't commit to love, I wasn't born with

enough love

I was not born to be loved and to love

So go, go far, run, run far, away, away, far away.

Don't turn back or you will be tempted.

For now, I have to fix myself, every inch of my shattered being

And take a taste at learning to love myself. I can't count on

anyone but me

Every day

My days were meaningless before you

Now I'm a unique person in meaningful days

Even if I can't be stable and you cannot see me

I am the wind waking up in a new direction

Blowing up a new person's life

With no idea where, what I could be tomorrow

And then tomorrow comes

Everything changes but one thing will never change

What we have striven to build and have

Our love is ambiguous and risky

It is doubtful, it is unsecured

It survives day to day with a little piece of hope and despair

Because it is hard for you

 to always fall in love again, again and again with an

indescribable being

It might be a rose today, but a resentful pine and lemongrass the

next day

But we know that it is there and will never go away even if I'm

gone today

My Muse

You are my muse,

You are my entertainment,

My distraction, you are the thing that I do to get away from

boredom.

My playground to learn about life.

The one and only thought that makes me wanna wake up in the

morning

And travel around the world, go to a wild journey with no

specific destination

With our love in my palms. I never want to let go of this

The only person that makes me wanna live

 in the moment with no worries of the future or the past.

Whenever we go, wherever you go, with me or without me,

 you will always find a home in my heart.

Sunny day of summer

I feel the hot sun burning down my heart that aches

The ice cream shop that I look at from far away

Watching the memories of us here

The park is so quiet in our habitual place

The noise of those little Birds singing our love in the green leaf

trees

And the little Squirrels running everywhere to pick at leftovers

My flowing dress that you sometimes catch in the back

The calm and the comfort that I found close to you

Laying down in the soft and chilly grass

And the sweetness of l'eau D'issey

 de cologne that I could not get enough from you

Suddenly I woke up, it is Winter

And I can't wait for Summer

<u>Nights</u>

Nights make us philosophers

Not of any subject but of our own lives

Nights are dark but the best time of enlightenment

Because they let us see what we've done

They let us give everything and we

don't have to hide anymore.

Nights are like careful mothers.

They just listen to our cries, listen to our suffering

They remind us of all the immoral actions

They show us the sides, the memories

of our true happiness, and the ones that we faked.

Nights let us be authentic,

 with no more fear. Nights are made to meditate

They are made to think about the past

the present and where and how to stand next.

Poetry

Poetry is my mirror

Poetry is the given pieces of me

It is my soul, my pain in meaningful

and undepictable words.

Poetry is my healer

Poetry shares my happiness, my expressions, my

Heartbreaks, my deep sorrows

Poetry is my comfort zone

It sheds my tears, it listens to me

Like the wind that flows in the quiet prairie

Like a baby that quiets down at the sight of mom

Me and Poetry is like Frida Kahlo's Self Portrait

Poetry never deceives, never betrays me.

Poetry keeps it all. All the unspoken words, all the anger.

Poetry is me, my soul. I don't trust anyone but Poetry

Rising

In the night sky

I see a beautiful glimmer of hope,

dazzling in the stars.

It holds a bright future

announcing open doors of eminent successes.

From here and now

I can see the journey to get there

Needing a real and optimistic smile.

It is the time to turn over a new green and fresh leaf

<u>Dear Pillow</u>

Dear pillow, thank you for always being there when I always

need it

I know I mostly needed you in my worst times. But you always

made them better

You took my every single tear drop filled with pains, struggles.

When I was feeling like disappearing. You covered my face with

your darkness because sometimes, I was tired of the world's light.

When I needed to yell out loud all the pain,

 you were there to allow me.

You listened to me peacefully, and let me release all pain.

About the Author

Born and raised in the West African country Burkina Faso, Windila Balbone is a strong ambitious young woman who writes to give voice to issues that matter. She moved to the USA in 2014 in search for a better quality of education. She graduated as the valedictorian of her high school class and will enroll in SUNY Potsdam in the Fall of 2017, where she plans to major in Creative Writing and Biology. She is the recipient of the 2017 President's Award for Academic Excellence. In addition to her stellar academic achievements, Windila continues to advocate for the less fortunate members of society. Her work with the International Rescue Committee and the Children Defense Fund won her praises as a change agent for the next generation.

Made in the USA
Middletown, DE
20 July 2017